www.finishinglinepress.com

BEASTING

poems by

Timothy Ree

Finishing Line Press
Georgetown, Kentucky

BEASTING

for my parents

Copyright © 2022 by Timothy Ree
ISBN 978-1-64662-930-5 First Edition
All rights reserved under International and Pan-American Copyright Conventions.
No part of this book may be reproduced in any manner whatsoever without written
permission from the publisher, except in the case of brief quotations embodied in
critical articles and reviews.

ACKNOWLEDGMENTS

Thank you to the following teachers, colleagues, or fellow writers who have
held direct sway over the image, substance, sonics, or the shape of my lines
toward some semblance of meaning over the years: Jill P. Baumgaertner,
Dianne Bilyak, Martha Serpas, Idra Novey, Joseph O. Legaspi, Eduardo C.
Corral, Brian Teare, Rachel Eliza Griffiths, Ruth Forman, Cheryl Savageau,
Danny Shot, Katie Naoum Rogers, Robin McCullough, Phyllis Witte,
Melissa Goodrum, Jonathan Scolnick, Joseph Garnevicus, Ashleigh A. Allen,
and Alana Mazur. Thank you Sam Swope and Rene Marion at the Academy
for Teachers for your vision and generous support along with the Bread
Loaf School of English. Thank you Yeon Ji Yoo for the stunning artwork.
Thank you to the few who kept up during the worst of the 'rona: Willem Lee,
Eunice Kwon, Constantine Tsiatsos, Hannah Joyce, Daniel Lee, and Sharon
Ree Ha. Thank you, finally, to the following publications—their readers and
editors—for listening first and for considering earlier drafts of these poems:

Bread Loaf School of English—Coke, Alone
Great Weather for Media—Pops the OG Maverick
Poets House—I Say Now These Are the Soul
The Cortland Review—Stations
Tribes—Family Portrait & Zoom Nation

Publisher: Leah Huete de Maines
Editor: Christen Kincaid
Cover Art: Yeon Ji Yoo
Author Photo: Timothy Ree
Cover Design: Elizabeth Maines McCleavy

Order online: www.finishinglinepress.com
            also available on amazon.com

Author inquiries and mail orders:
Finishing Line Press
P. O. Box 1626
Georgetown, Kentucky 40324
U. S. A.

Contents

I. [Left Panel]

"Listen, I tell you a mystery:
We will not all sleep, but we will all be changed."
                                                —Paul

Dinner with George

Tonight, the world reeks of Raid
                    the hush of ants on a windowsill

like spilled vinegar on
                    the marble top, like chopped scallions.

I open the fridge
                    for once: watch me eat these frozen flakes of milk.

The bottom of an empty bottle of Laphroaig
                              my go-to, to crush the blow
                        in the baggie.

          In the hall an occasional beeping: soon the death
of a smoke detector.

          Laughter somewhere, a fork grazing a plate. With whom
will I dine tonight

          but you, George, my Venus Flytrap? You and a floor fan
and a handful of hair

          inching up the dark linoleum. Sometimes
I fear a living room

                    this room full of Jack-in-the-boxes: in unison
their metal cranks turning to the tune

                    of ice-cream trucks, having to kneel naked
among them, these tin boxes, waiting for one of them

                    to out himself as Lord.

Last Night

A roach the size of a squirrel
                              nibbling your knee. Kick hard the horror

heaving dark thing across
                    the room. No roach, relax, no squirrel-

as-roach.
              Your neighbor says he'd been pounding for hours.

Others
          behind him: twenty, thirty in the hall, in their hooded sweatshirts.

Your last night here
                    believe. A row of pointy hoods nodding, swaying,

a soft cackling,
                then several, louder, then nothing. Close the door

on your future.
              Someone nudging it open, whispers *Ready*
                                            or not, you are ready.
Turn, grab the first hoody
                    from a drawer full of hoodies. Step out barefoot

onto marble, into
              a slow march down the hall. You're pulling up

the rear.
          Dark shapes scuttle by on the floor, weave in and out the line

of bare feet. Careful not
              to step, to pulp them to a crush.

Questions for My Body (1/3)

After Eduardo C. Corral

Have you given up on
        the moist book of matches?

Have you learned yet to call a cavern
        a cavern?

Do you still hear in your head
        the owls? Why is it always

inside your mind
        so humid? What did you want with her

lower left molar? Did
        you want more the hole

the tooth left, to tongue
        your nestle into dark spaces?

Are those nose rings or earrings
        under your tongue?

Coke, Alone

It is horchata-cloudy this morning
                    with a chance   of amputation

meaning it's slightly humid, meaning
                    my lines may be difficult to parse.

The barber is out for months, his car
                    t-boned   at some intersection

in Vermont. Glass everywhere
                    they said   even in his mouth.

They found me inside his nostrils
                    like white pebbles on a dry riverbed

like lint dotting the lining
                    of a winter coat. Who's to blame

for such cavernous sadness, for speed
                    through stop signs & hidden lights?

Soon I've smuggled myself in, snow
                    on a frozen lake, a mirror in which you

behold your own beauty, on which
                    you too might shatter a nose.

Questions for My Body (2/3)

Where within you

        is that finger you swallowed?

Which veins contain her? Why

        her collarbone? Whom else

have you beasted

        on a street corner? Were there two

or three gold rings on

        that finger you ate? Is it mostly day

or night in your ear canal? Why

        do you still smell of kerosene?

Who healed you

        of the fungus? Whose nails growing in place

of yours? Who

        has skunked so suddenly your hair?

Restocking the Fridge

The olives, the dates, in this light

                         are roaches I'd been saving

for hard times. Are these almonds or the tips

                     of your fingers?

Do almonds go in the fridge?

               Do onions? Groceries for once. All

these chores I've been neglecting all my life

                    like eating, sleeping.

A table

      of unopened bills, the unpeeled sticker on a credit card

replacement,

        the Swiffer more hassle than mop. The sun is moon

in a few hours.

        I'm hanging my old skin

                  on the clothesline—pass me

a clothespin—

        it will loosen throughout the night, in the dew

of the early morning.

        I'll need it tomorrow—my skin, my old

squid—to sallow

        the world as I am, as I've always been, swimming

or drowning

        or a third thing in this light, a new thing, I tell you a mystery.

Questions for My Body (3/3)

Do you want at times
                    to bleed, to blade her out?

How long would it be, all your veins
                              into a taut line?

Long enough for a round
                    of double dutch?

What bars would you spit while
                              swinging the rope?

How many drinks
              to unswing Anne from the chandelier?

Are you the cannon or the one
                        inside the cannon?

Whose wife, whose mother
                    or why of late this cannibal?

Is that on your outer
                left thigh the scar left

from the burning tent?
                    Which parts of your body

have you never
              seen? What if someone were dying now

or thinking of dying?

Stations

Blood from the showerhead

                or rusty water—hard to tell

      in the early blue.

        ■

On the train

    a man reading a Bible—

            its cover a brown camouflage.

        ■

The blonde who got on tall

         at *Parkside*—with sunglasses,

     no ring.

        ■

I'm chasing a coffee napkin down the street, past a hydrant

    painted stars and stripes—

           this early, this much to bear.

        ■

Someone this hour, in this city

        is just as drunk—puts a lit cigarette

    in his coat pocket.

        ■

In the elevator

    to feel like meat in a freezer—soon the flies,

                the children.

        ■

No—
       the room crowded with squirrels, each one
                            completely still.

■

Now a lesson on metaphors: soon
                   they will all be mixed—
I am the gate, you are the branches . . .

■

Once on the sidewalk
          we were mugged by falling acorn—
one of us stabbed with a beak.

■

There
      not the stolen wheel, the fallen chain—
         but the good frame left hanging on the iron arch.

■

In the empty square my way home,
        a phone vibrating on a stone chess table—
sound and riddle of our lives.

■

Now for the local
      or the express—the express to the local back
                    one stop.

■

Someone this hour, in this city
        is kneeling—another
                 receiving.

■

To scroll down the glow—
the list
of useless names.

Moonlight Sonata

You playing   the left-hand part

with a foot.   Then your big toenail

falls off   slips into the dark slit

between   piano keys. A low C# jams.

■

Get off the pedal   your pa pops.

Pump the pedal, more precisely.   Ain't

no pedal in the opening.   Connect

them eighth notes   you fool, you idiot.

■

But check it   you ain't pressing

no pedal.   When you stand up

to leave   the note still hums

down the hallway   for days.

■

The same pitch   of a bell

tolling   white hot, sky high.

You somewhere   in England.

Some skeletal   cathedral.

■

No dome   no stained glass.

Long patch   of grass where

the aisle used to be   flanked

by flowers   instead of pews.

■

Check it   construction

all around   scaffolding

like a ribcage & bet   your own heart

bloating somewhere   inside.

■

Son   a naked descent! Boy

be sliding down   a wet pole

from the roof   of the refectory.

It's all   gravity, skin, laughter.

■

You   naked in the living room.

A violin bow comes down on your crown

snaps   in half. My son

check it, you got   blonde hair!

■

Your pop's already there.   Yells out

something   bout real horsehair, antique wood.

Your sister   be yelling, now crying.

Pa pops off   sends you to your room.

■

Behold, the silhouette of your own sleeping body

you writhing fish   in the dark hull of a boat.

Reach for the dial   turn down the loud

Ludwig van.   Lay a palm, calm the dreaming child.

Waiting for You at a Bar Pre-Covid

Girl quotes lines from my own poem after class: *It is horchata-cloudy this morning / with a chance of amputation.* You're not just a teacher, she says. Found you online.

■

This waitress, her pizza slice earrings pointing down to the ground where I'd bury my rage, where I'd bury. I'll take a beer and a shot, for now.

■

Before you arrive, I write our initials on the chalkboard wall, in the bathroom, with pink nub of chalk the size of a pinky tip.

■

I want the full length of your freckled leg down my throat. I want to gag, to make myself throw you up in the wet-solid mess of these poems.

■

Today, I slap-killed a roach the size of my kneecap with a clear plastic clipboard. The thing split open like a lobster, white flesh smeared all over the dark hardwood.

■

In lieu of body bag, two or three tissues I lay over the body and, as I closed my hand over it, it felt warm. Or was it my brain imposing warmth, imposing a body?

■

I want a close-up cam inside your mouth, along with an MRI brain-scanning chart-activity for when you're gathering saliva for your hand for my cock.

■

That gathering-spit moment, those seconds I want to slow down, I want to understand. We'll order, within the hour, a basket of fries with a side of mayo.

■

When you do arrive. If you do arrive. And then you are here.

I Say Now These Are the Soul

After Walt Whitman

How the hell it got here, in the apartment   behind
        this ugly couch we're so tired of looking at—the leg.

      ■

Imagine the rest of it   the rest of them naked   bald—
      mannequins in the room   seated by old typewriters
    clicking word by slow word   late into the night.

      ■

Once   in a show on TV   up past midnight when I had
      the chance   the horror wasn't the dark curly wig
but the slow strange crawl across the kitchen floor.

      ■

How parts of us move   grow   despite us detach—
      like mercy   like the idea of mercy
    withheld from those who need it most.

      ■

A kaleidoscope the size of a finger   forgotten toy
      looking through it to blood cells to flowers on fire
    the inner dome of a cathedral   to stars.

      ■

All I see now   is a landscape of bone
      as in *Where were you pointing, pops? Where*
                           exactly?

      ■

My favorite blue yo-yo   O the moves I'd master:
          the loop-the-loop, the sleeper   the dreamer become
          a dog on a leash become a baby in a cradle   rocking—

■

The flying saucer   or the man on a flying trapeze—
          had I practiced enough—   had we not outgrown wonder.
                    The Eiffel Tower made of string.

■

Remember grinning   first time flipping through
          the legend   I whispered *No, a headless horse*
or a horse with a missing leg.

■

In *The Seventh Seal*   how the knight stares at his hand
          same hand with which he has, for now, evaded Death—
at chess, what else?

■

That he can move it   that he
                    can move it at will—
          miracle enough.

■

We left it for you   the leg by the curb.
          We slipped it   between two garbage bags.

Trail Running Pre-Covid

The weight and foot placement paranoia when running down trails in the dark this early, earlier than birds or squirrels or salamanders. Not trying to sprain an ankle.

∎

The fog hovering over the field obscuring the dog walkers, above or below. More precisely, cutting their legs off leaving their torsos. Or, more mercifully, decapitating them.

∎

The hem of the toilet paper just visible in the stall beside me, to pull from this roll—that kind of audacity—instead of sheepish request.

∎

What is being masked, as in, masking tape? These exposed steaming pipes, at least, my view while peeing in a stall. Maybe I should mask my face further before my next class.

∎

The tree-stump altar, table now for squirrels or vapers or drinkers. How many webs will I face-first run into this afternoon looking for lost children, looking for discs?

∎

I'm thinking grits and beer for lunch in the square. A brown leaf just dropped and landed, a bird, it turns out. We're old beef now with freezer burn, aren't we, some guy says, the beef of our bodies.

∎

The dream where I'm pressing against the door through which women want to enter because, well, we're in their room, presumably, naked and ashamed. If they'd all come in. They do come in, one after another, all my female co-workers.

■

Not the tortoise nor the hare, but the moose that just moved, distinguishing itself from the trees in the background of the story. Now it's a race to skin or to shell each of these alive.

■

A trail through the woods reserved for horses, we walked toward a tree older than anyone we remember, the parents of our grandparents, for example. We bent down to smell the droppings, their fragrance.

■

The base of the oak the width of a twin bed. How coarse the bark, as if stripped of its bedsheets. We're pressed against each other on this bed.

■

To verbify tourniquet in some future poem combined with, if possible, a burning harp or a purple thumbprint or a drawer full of lizard tails, all the ones we learned to live without.

At Last, Terror Has Arrived

After Arda Collins

And the squirrels as well, thousands
                marching double-file down 6th Avenue

which means something is burning
                someone is burning.

Sound in the alley of a cat in heat
                or a child hanging, swaying, his head caught

in the chain net on the otherwise
                empty asphalt—this sound.

I'm swallowing a handful of tacks
                because the voice in the head

of a man in my head is telling us
                the tacks are Skittles from last year's Halloween

the one umma warned
                us of, shutting all the blinds, turning off the lamps.

She's lighting the tip of her finger
                to light a page of a book from which

we draw wisdom tonight.
                At last, terror has arrived.

Umma sputtering, humming her favorite
                hymn, as she burns slowly down

as we huddle closer from what outside these walls
                would devour us.

II. [Center Panel]

". . . in a flash, in the twinkling of an eye, at the last trumpet. For the trumpet will sound, the dead will be raised imperishable, and we will be changed."

—Paul

Family Portrait

After James Allen Hall

When I say my moms
                 I mean I slip Jesus in my mouth—

a slab of white chocolate
                 sucking slow, sweetly

the saliva doing its work toward
                 the razor blades.

When I say my pops
                 the pipes begin again

their heat-clamor
                 the praise-latest of radiators the sound

of Covid-pneumonia.
                 I'm in the family dining room, the tablecloth

a light-green linen—
                 a freshly mown, tear-gassed field.

I'm writing by light of bourbon
                 and the late-night glow

of poached eggs. Soon, the sun
                 through the wooden Venetians

will make of this room
                 a jail cell. I'll be sleeping upright

in my father's usual spot, the head
                 of this table. Picture

the purple dogwood-explosion
                 through the window

behind me, and the bats huddling within—
                 the bats we'll learn to beast.

After Lucille Clifton

Won't you celebrate
with me
what I

have stitched
into a kind
of life?

I, too
had no model.
See where

I split, where
I suture
daily, slip

into a kind
of skin
worth wearing.

Listen now
to more
than violins

more
than violas or cellos
of darker wood.

Listen
to the clarinets doused
in cold milk

or the lone oboe
in the alley [listen]
beside a burning bin [listen]

or a flute
in the stairwell [listen] leading
to an attic.

Listen
from whichever rooms
imprison you.

See the wind
through a forest of swaying
bassoons

cut down
and riddled by rubber bullets,
the bells

of all
the trumpets dented
by batons.

The world
is painful-gorgeous, and I
feel infinite

within it because
of two portabella mushrooms
glazed

with basil
and roasted garlic-hot resplendent
out the oven

this evening.
Won't you celebrate
with me

the measured rests
amid bluer
notes

as everyday
someone has tried
to fiddle me

to rip the seams of my lips
open
and has failed.

Your Name on My Phone Is Hieronymus Bosch

Last night

I lost a finger

but I found it

in the dark

puddle, floating

like a dead fish.

It was

already

purpling. I

re-attached it bone

on bone

like re-reeding

a clarinet. I tried

making a fist

and just like that

I was healed.

Temple Asphyxiation

I came twice with you / I split / with the blade of me / the apricot

you gave me / I ravaged one half / the juice cascading my lower lip /

the other I squeezed into a flattened thing / bleeding it first of its nectar

then made of it / a fruit cockring / to dance / on the strobe-lit floor

of your childhood of hand-me-down toys / the yo-yo / silver slinky /

finger cuffs / kaleidoscopes the size of our fingers / as whatever we

pointed out was prism-lit geometry of joy / like a cubist Grand Canyon

say / a Caldered mobile of a red mobile / listen / let me unbutton my

chest / so you might leap-gazelle down my valleys & canyons / into bat

laden caves / your face is a dartboard or a baseball target / an oiled

mitt / hold that shit up / choose / thine own adventure / killer shrimp

or murdered by a savage swarm of guppies / stomped on by a giraffe

or coiled tight by a blue python / death by / stalactite through the eye

or stalagmite through the temple / asphyxiation by blue birthday balloon

or slip off the edge into steaming magma / death metal Abu Ghraibish

or a small finch feather / tickling the arch of your footbed / like I said

choose thine own adventure / death by Covidiocy / or a knee kneading

your sourdough neck then shoveled into oven / ass-bat bitten in your

sleep / or police baton to the pelvis at the noon of your life / belly-relegated for hours / what your silence sometimes feels like / swoop

into stalactites / stalagmites / my rodent face impaled / a wing ripped

off like a piece of beef jerky / a flag with a bird-shaped hole through

which a thousand bats tunnel through / in broadly lit afternoon in mid-

July / like a tin can of hand salve / stuck shut no longer speaking &

softening my skin / a brush / a hairbrush / on this dining room table

/ all these grays / all these straight up whites / to whom now will I

direct my rage?   Lord / the air be apricots this morning.

Yes, Yes

To sniff the musk of your armpits, lick
>   your pits and graze

the prickly skin of kiwis.
>   I wake instead to a handful of cherries, one

a deep maroon, two of brighter
>   red, then three both sorrow

and joy I choose, if
>   you're offering, this morning. How many dogs ago

were we wolves? How bout we amble
>   the ask of the day down a hallway

of sunflowers? I ramble
>   like mold greening the beef jerky, this motley bag

of almonds, raisins, granola embedded
>   in dark chocolate we'll beast

by the creek, the flies with squirrel jaws going
>   for our earlobes, our thighs.

Pinecones the size of babies
>   how horrendous and gorgeous. Creep, deer, into

the cave of my grey hoodie, hear
>   the bats rustling in my lungs, hanging

for now on my ribs. I need your palm glazed
>   with sunflower oil, flecked

with basil, your piston grip slow
>   then savage fast till I bloom into bouquet—

a whole field
>   of moonlit flowers on my belly.

Isaias Rolls Up on America

All these amputated fists, femurs.
                              Wind guillotines

and straight beheadings, these
                              orphaned leaves all beauty

in their savage. Meanwhile
                              the sun, as usual, don't give

a flying fish, is
                    smirking-hot brightly with its choir of white

hooded clouds.
                    Not swaying because, well, they can't

dance, singing
                    their German hymns. The water, heil. Hightide

has drug up
              the skiffs, the bloated boats   up onto the eye-level

bay. They'll need to grow
                              some goddamn legs right quick

if the water spills
                    all up on the streets   a gospel-drown gagging

we've had
          to gargle since the flood.   My bullyhuff and puff

to blow
          their brick-shit down.   Behold, the four

leafy beasts
              writhing now   in the wind.

My Gazelle Goes on a Stroll by the Bay

Machine my cog.   Pave my tar.

Nothing more   resplendent

than two robins   one flattened

the other still pulsing   breathing

its warm red ribcage on the freshly

tarred street let me   ride on by

this morning   toward the harbor

how savage the day.   Inside the water

are waves   within waves

of cold of lukewarm   like the water's own

urination colors   and light

golden coins that   darkness that abyss

the throat of the earth that gorgeous brown

pinstripe suit I left in the hotel closet

in Saltsjobaden.   Roach now for

a pair of socks a new   pair of feet from

some random-ass moment in your life.

We remove our feet   we

cut them off nightly   grope

for them the next morning by texture

by scent of semen   alone. Choose

thine own feet. I got   only one hand on

the handlebar, the one without a brake.

Your hemisphere, you said, is sending

the heat our way.   Creature, you

too, this hour-elixir   of smooth roads

with our road bikes?   Ring the fucking bell.

Squirrel in my hammock just chilling

this morning.   You'll bite

your own nostril   meaning, you got

a nose piercing, you've flutified your face.

Home is a door through the door

through the door   through the door

the blood-slathered   wooden door.

Self Portrait in Bacurau, Bowling Shirt, and Gat

Wave the white linen in the air for me too
when I die, my crane unfolded, the flag of me
unfurled and deported
       into the August wind. O
snap, listen now the bass, the synthesizer
70s style, grounding everything we've never
flown on the front lawn,
       old glory un-triangled,
like a country fraying and going to shams, shitake
mushrooms roast-boiled and pureed by recipe
imperial.
    Don't fuck up, my father used to say,
the first button-mismatch on your favorite blue
shirt, the bowling shirt you got in second grade
from the Army
      Salvation on 5th Ave, north Philly,
how I loved that shitty shirt. Now, all I want is
a sleek black gat made, I'm told, of horsehair
and bamboo—
      they'd boil the bamboo, slice it
into hair-like strands—we'd zip to Zapf's music
for valve oil, some salve for our impoverished
lives, some gospel for our
       trumpeting ignorance—
they'd weave and shape-caress it by hand, these
hands that have touched so many wet things, so
many clits, cocks,
      countless my engorged childhood
alone—months, on average, to yield a single
gat, whose hands, these hands—to make of
these tentacles
      a double-dutch rope, swinging
double on its own, through the Philly wind, chilly
the willow limbs no longer languorous, meaning,
somewhere there are leaves,

                           limbs blown off
like gats the white wind snatches from off
our heads. How pristinely we've been folded—
creased, tendered tight
                           origami, into birds, into
hats, into our favorite shirts we'll be buried in
soon—in Bacurau. We be under siege forever
by the true
          blue code of sky, of silent bullet-brutal
minutes, days, and all the years left ahead.

Notes on Enneagram 8w7 :: The Maverick

Auto-rebellion.
Auto-rebellious, vengeance.

Why   the gas bill so high? Why   be pickles all up in my burger?
Who's to blame? De-victimize me. De-center the pizza pie, let the buffalo wings in.

I grow. I engorge. So tight the gorge, so steep-walled on either side we have the sun
an hour tops   I hate   deceit, and our deceits are not the same.

Not waking up brooding approval of my trumpet solo. I can end a fight, as in
bring it, fool, I'll fucking finish you   murder you   with a mouthpiece.

Lust, sin   for my purpose gluttony   combined, makes for
a force, a fifth of Laphroaig no lie   every night for thirty-six moons, yo.

Wreck me. Try to reckon me, try. Pulse me. Won't you join in my vision of auto-
rebellion? Nah. I be dropping   pearls, but pearls in their snouts be lodged.

Bro, eat shit before I ever oink for help   from any of you.   Oink me why
I'm wrong.   Pork me why your pigsty, a room   with all them useless books.

They do do, the 8s, before they think.   Who's to blame?   Tell me.
Does it warrant a pause   on the reel? Does it warrant   a pause, officer Thao?

Not that they do do (not shitting bulls) but that they prone to ride their hot air
balloons   sky cocoons over   a tear-gassed America, ready to drop the Asian.

My deceit   is not your deceit. My bear isn't picking a fight. Are y'all prepared?
Are y'all adequate? I'm smiling, but judging your ass-cracker coward, I dare you.

The underdog. The dog under the dog bark behind the bark of the dying tree.
I'm an 8   so trumpet your own   motherfucking truth.

Is this a fight I need to be in now? Be, what, present to life? Bitch please, I used
to say. Do I need   to put my bulldog down? Put the bark back in my face?

Thanks, Dr. LaHue or *I Use LaHue to Write a Poem.* The color of your beard
is the hue of my doghead husky.   My doctor. Foster me now, my general.

Famous 8s include the Donald, Fidelio, the Joey Stalin, the midget-ass Napoleon,
Saddam, but also FD Roosevelt, Butterfly Ali, Spy Connery, and Paulie Picasso.

Banter is the test of your already
insider fort.

Wedding Banquet

I mean your sternum-ravine, to meet you
on persimmon path.
                              I wake intermittently
as the taut sharkskin of me arches, makes
an arc toward the cove of you through
this narrow entrance into an emerald oval
pool where
                    I'll rise gradually to the surface,
my fin fanning against the first air of the air
of the white-hot sky of my eventual finning
and, discarded,
                    still pulsating while sinking,
settling to the bed of the silty bay to be torn at
again by predators, by soup peddlers who'll
heat and boil me
                    into a stew for the wedding
banquet. Birds of a flock feather together
but lizard leather is more my skin, my
syncopated pores, my hexagonal music.
How many tails have we stowed in the dark
wooden drawer?
                    How many have we bitten off
or deeply throated? Inside this salmon is the tail
of a lizard, Lord, pass me the lotion made of
organic wildrose.
                    I'll take a shower now with
my black ankle socks on. I'll wade in the water
like a fucking moose.

The Circus Animals' Desertion

Or   *Yeats Be Trump Too.*   Kneecap
the postal service   with donkey jawbone, yes.

This guy   this urine-skin   is at it
again, the foreskin   of a nation state.

Me?   I shit out my d, pee out
my ass   when I eat out   the Lady

and the Tramp. Meanwhile, bone marrow.
Mara   Asian elephant been delivered

from carceral zoo   to carceral reservation,
Brazil. Follow me my animal   logic. I'm

its anchor baby   with my stutter-stuck jaw
as a kid, my   flap-howling   jowls, too—

check it, when I'm old and gray nodding not by
the fire.   Mara, ya circus beast

who bled out the gaze   of ya circus master.
Dare now thine own desertion!   Back to

the bone   foul bro, Billy Yeats, to the bone-
shop of your heart-   rags back, yes

to the bottom of the iron   spiral ladder.
What can we   but enumerate old themes

to make America gush again   from
its spongy parts   the marrow, the Maras

of today, tomorrow.   The mask become
a muzzle   become a filter system we'll use

on this three-day hike   to take this copper-
colored creek piss   and turn it clear.

Bells, Drums, Hiccups This Morning

Nothing more offensive than a loose snare drum
or church bells across

              the street playing a hymn
with a fortress their mighty god bells this hour
I have the hiccups I've

              got the hooks far gone
down my throat past rows and throes of spades
blades I have shoveled

              through so much useless
soil silt soda cans I've straight swallowed holy
shit you fist my anal mouth

              tunnel past my drowning
voice your soft white palm grazing jagged stones
like a salmon toward

              two hooks in my throat one
white hot metal the other a matte black both have
gagged me all my mother

              flinching life of slit eyes
open always in saltwater scanning the world-womb
the rooms I've predatored

              with the pitch nuance the
hue-rhythms of silence. You can't unring a bell
meaning I'm sorry love

              meaning you may maim my
bell tongue or remove the hooks let me swim
toward you and nestle

              your inner thighs—
              let me sleep there this morning.

Mushrooms

After Sylvia Plath

Breathe in the sky   like a cigarette in Cali
a whiff of Minnesota   a long drag of Wisconsin.

Shrooms on this trail   these dark wooden tables
and plates   skin of red lizards   brown

spotted leopards   furless, too, these slate-grey
hammerhead sharks   here blue, snakeskin smooth

with hexagonal braille.   Sylvia, sister, listen :: we shall not
inherit shit. We'll take back   what was stolen.

The most beautiful ones   be the most deadly, bet.
Check this   an upside-down mushroom

is a chandelier   my friend Anne hung herself from.
Anne   the chandelier of our nights. I wanted

to swallow all those swallows   on that new shirt
they said they   found her in. Quiet as fuck

for really   there is no they, no collective hour, our
nothing. Alone   with their toes, their sharp

noses, but everyone sees you now   feels your
small grains, hidden gains   the rooms you've fungused

for years. Don't front :: the meek   shall never
inherit the earth   no female, no male

but folx, foxes with   their rough gnarled
fists   even the severed ones   still twitching on

the pavement   their middle fingers stabbing
what's left of the day, what's left   of the air.

Hammer home   their ram-headers against the black
top   parking lot. So many of you, so many still silent

nudgers, shovers on the sidewalk   doing shit, taking
vids. We shall   by mourning inherit the dead

and the dead are still edible, bet.   We'll start like dogs
at their feet.

Taxidermy

A sheep-colored rug rolls off a pickup truck ahead and we swerve around the unraveling animal thing. I slow down as we pass to look for its eyes.

■

Once, with my needle-point pen, I carved our names into the wooden wall of a bathroom, watercolor fish on the light-green wallpaper. Behold, my fishbowl view. Even painting is a kind of taxidermy.

■

Montage of all the deer selfies you've ever sent me on loop-boomerang projected, as in a theater, the screen my bare left chest, your mouth opening and closing with cameo-tongue in sync-rhythm to my heartbeat, beating off meanwhile my own antlers despite you now, my blue truth-ache. I should delete this hidden folder, this hiddenness.

■

In the dream I leave you at the marketplace arcade, then return immediately for regret. By then you were gone, and I kept screaming your name, a name the janitor, the merchants, even the sous chefs dressed in white began parroting. All the white parrots.

■

My dark brown-black I mistook for a deer, I fear a deer dark brown-black charred during times of smoke and ash and feathers laced with blow, like ash, ash we're sniffing now, as the world turns toward its own grave.

■

Chipmunks everywhere in these woods or shifting leaves. Chasing the cotton-ball of a brown bunny through brown bamboo shoots, presumable bunny. Not sure if it were a bunny's tail I followed, but I did follow the white comet through a bamboo galaxy.

■

Into wood, into sand, into chalkboard our initials, D.D. & S.S.—or Dear Deer and Salmon Says. Salmon says lift a hoof. Salmon says lift your antlers. Now cut off your antlers. Salmon says you need me. Salmon says you love me. You love me, dear deer.

■

Albino deer exist after all, or a waft of fog. So do black squirrels. They exist, says Google images. My friend's live picture-portrait, her side-eye and point of view pan to her bed where her fox-looking dog is taxidermic-still.

■

The stillness of ants, sometimes, when I've turned on the bathroom light, having thumb-pressed the slower ones on the sink. I'll leave em like that, them dots on display.

■

Is that a crushed pinecone or an upturned roach on the road? Either way it's moving, and it's moving away, wind-skittering off or on its own. We'll take the Taconic home.

Pops the OG Maverick

Hawk / goes my hawk / pops / flown / to the bathroom

this hour / hawk-yawp / cross the freshly carpet-stripped

oak / hawk / through a glass darkly hammers / its beak-face

shatters through twilight window / drag-leading other birds

and bats / gamey-together up / from his lungs up his throat

all up on / the summit of his tongue / hawk-perch / a hawk /

hawk / this heaven of hawk / this hell of a hawk this heaving

hour / head out to see now / if he needs water / he's good /

head out for a walk / obsessing poems about fish fish-bait

& hooks / the fishers more obviously y'all / we / the people

we the hooks say / at least five kinds / says the fish kiosk by

the pond the arboretum this holy hour might bring my nieces

post vaccine / post Covid in Chief come November / leaves

on the trail just be dead / fish who dared step out the pond /

mugshots of fish / arrows pointing left / police line-up / ya

common carp / ya koi / ya green sunfish & large-mouth bass

/ bluegill & check it / channel catfish we / the people / we

the hooks too / at least in this pic in this corner / at least five

kinds of hook-threat / if you consider color / a matte black or white / shiny silver bet / increasing variations / of curve

& coil & loopback ridges / edges to snag more of my tongue-

throat / with whipsaw effort of blacks / whites to red-sever

my vocal cords / to hawk & talon my koi right out / this pond

/ this hawk claw plunge down my father's throat the pond

of his lungs / be fishers of men white men be preaching since

the start / of the sermon of men / hook line & sinker not ever

for women / is how I hear them preachers now / with hook

in my mouth my inner cheek / snag dragged as I writhe savage

floppin dry in the October wind / dry my scales / my clothes

final tug-snap of fins before / I'm hung up / on the laundry line

like a beige towel / ojingeo twigim / or the darker green of gim

/ autumn leaves in the wind what I'm saying is that my pop's

been violated in this country & I wasn't always there to stop it

what I mean is / I love him what I mean is / I'm thinking hard

on his death maybe I'm thinking too of language / once my pops

heaved out of our blue station wagon to hawk some road rage /

a white man gave him the finger / & pops wasn't havin it.

Heat Lightning

After Carl Phillips

Less, not more lucidity, is what we were praying for, then. Preying.

Who says despair is belief's true echo? Who says, my lovely mantis?

I believe in my father, the son, and the approaching storm.

Sure, my pops be saying, you unoriginal fool.

He goes, Check out Symphony no. 6, talking bout storms.

No *e pluribus unum*, for a time, anyway, of pansori rhymes.

Beethoven was, too, toward the end, some even say, a blind-ass mofo. A bat.

Let's take his shit, mix it with our own, and hear what thunders next.

Let's close the windows of this cave.

III. [Right Panel]

> "Where, O death, is your victory?
> Where, O death, is your sting?"
>
> —Paul, after Hosea

The Persistence of Memory (After Dali)

Three clocks / freshly fried haemul pajun my moms made

every Sunday morning before the desert of church / a fourth

lone kimchi jun covered by then with ants / flies all around

the stove / we'd reach for the red plastic fly swatter look here

in the center the carcass of our prayers / check them fake

long lashes on a dying sea lion or a seal whatnot walrus dying

beast of my pops / will I have to dig him a solid / a grave

in the sand / slip / lo / his tongue back into his mouth what

slow muttering would snail from his face in the end? Once

pops & I drove by an absent seaside / we bet the August rain

subsiding soon / saw the darker sand shifting back to bright

right quick / the beach kicking off its cloud covers toward

the sea meaning time we pull up & park / find an empty table

a bar / where else could we drink & not think about decay?

Halloween, Bergen County

Giant brown-black hairy tarantulas palming all their roofs /

all their pumpkins carved out into Covid-heads / slit-eyed

Chinese chomping live bats / could just buy / some cheap-

ass bats from the dollar-party store / a scarecrow party on

the lawn of school children or old midgets waiting to die /

yo / can this persona right here / say midgets / say Covid-

head gooks right now / these chinks / these japfuck nips /

them zipper-head dinks / let's press our pale palms together

konichiwa style / bow / greet these scarecrows / can't tell

by what they wearing / if they be young or old / if they be

dead / can't even front now / for the dumbest flap of crows

cawing murder above / murdered men / women / judging

from the height of those skeletons / murder / not suicide

judging by the hoist-high dangling in the oak / folks out for

some gleesome lynching / say instead of all the skeletons

we took out this year / arranged into waltz or square dance

clever positions / instead / check it / we go giant fishbone

skeletons upright / playing they own ribs like harps / hoe-

down shimmy out the pond at long last / dancing the grave

out their own pain & joy / look up at toilet paper ghouls

wafting tops of trees / behold / six tourniquet / tree-stump

stools / huddled around a black plastic cauldron / double

double / such toil & trouble this year / this horizon / bet

a witch on a broom / no / instead of a broom someone's

leg / no instead of a leg bassoon of deep maroon / clarinet

/ a flute the size of a forearm / yo / more witches riding by

no-hands on they brooms / playing piccolo-shins to the tune

of ice-cream trucks / all roads lead / to lit Jack-o-lanterns /

toward violence and vision / to a lawn in Fairlawn of buried

bodies & heads / hands jutting up still praising from the dead.

Zoom Nation

Keep your cameras on if you are X / if you are Y keep
your cam on / if you Z keep thy body cams on them
cops with your copeyes / no copouts kids / ain't no bigger

fry to fish / you wish we was in person don't ya / ya wish
we was outdoors / more stream than fish is what I mean
streaming not at all savage down this once raging gorge /

from above my mask I cop a feel / your black g-string
under your white skorts / as you mount that jagged stone /
just a few more steps till we smash the summit / knock

our boots all up on them smoother wind scorched stones /
keep your cameras on at the ready / airplane mode so ya
don't drain the juice / for whatever found art on these

trails / the feet / no the feeling of daddy long legs the back
of my neck / the light acupuncture a half pitch higher
than the sun's grazing slow burn of my body / this body

bag a redundant phrase / when we hear the thump of
the body just tipped over the side of this stone throne /
as some of us when the world is too steep / too steeped

in shit would slither zig zag up the trail / some would
march straight through the granite / but most would turn
the fuck around / turn it off for X / for Y and Z / behold

a swarm of gnats / through this haze the beige shift of
a deer just beyond them trees / the shimmer of a spider web /
a hovering red dragonfly / a blue tail on a black salamander.

Blessed Assurance [or My Moms the High Priest Preaches on 1 Chronicles 20 after the Opening Hymn]

Supposed dude with six fingers on each hand   six toes on each foot.

Nah, I think. Six toes on each hand   six fingers on each foot. Phalanges

in other words   & Picasso, who else? Be a wet leaf, she lulls, so Satan

the wind does not snatch thee   from off the sidewalk. Thereby survive

them fires & earthquakes, tear gas protest   & virus riots, as the wind

(still Satan) shall not sweep us   into oblivion. Stay blessed, y'all, wet leaf

assurance & sticky till the end, my moms be preaching.   Bet. No, behold

a moonlit knife   the night of a star chef or the rapist in chief, just so

this Covid night of our Lord Jesus Christ   or Lucifer, lo, toward

salvation or suicide   the beastly disease of divorce, say, all manner of

extinction   goes the high priest preaching on what, now, this holy hour?

This ain't my story, this ain't my song.   O what a foretaste of gory divine.

Hannah Has the Covid

Close your eyes / start a poem with the sounds / where blindness

might lead us / unmute to a sudden waterfall / a marble hallway

full of mice / maybe / the cave-loud echo of bats / hundreds /

thousands / a seagull-swarm / mobbing a day-old carcass of a

beached beluga / this sound / sound / of a dozen hawks diving

hard onto a dying black bear / the meat of her fly-riddled / belly

split open & oozing out her future / eyes open now / eruption

of blackbirds / mini witches the tips of their brooms their sharp

beaks / the style of their flapping tells us no / they ain't / they

can't be bats / they be black swallows bet / their swoop & turn

of wings like a school of minnows / school kids / in the cafeteria

them squealing bats / raucous seagulls / no them mice gnawing

away at the roadkill deer / fore / look out / a full-on forest brawl

flapping / beak-stabbing & claw-talon destroying one another /

meaning Hannah has the Covid / I'm in the pews now / moms

with her blue tambourine / slapping her right hip / her hallelujahs

heaving into the mic / the hymn at high volume / pop / puffing

we hear her huff-inhale in prep for the next measure / measure

our lives by how we heave hallelujahs despite our charred lungs /

our sharp crown invisible virus stab-hooking / ripping & scraping

the inner walls / our painted caves flicker-lit / scenes of dancing

ancestors / hands-held around a fire / the swallows / the bison /

the deer / the bow & arrow / arrowhead spears into our hearts /

the threats / hallelujah / have always across ages / been the same.

Triptych [or Jesus Says, According to Matt 24 : 4—14]

watch out	[that no one deceives]	you
for	many [will come] in my name	claiming
I am the Messiah	[and] will deceive [many	
you will hear	of wars and rumors	of wars but
see	to it that] you [are not alarmed	
such things	must happen but	the end is still
to come	nation] will rise [against	
nation and kingdom	against kingdom there will] be	
famines	[and] earthquakes in	
various	[places all these are	the beginning of
birth pains	then	
you will	be handed over to	
be persecuted	and put	
to death	and] you [will] be	
hated by all	nations [because	
of me	at that time many will	
turn away from	the faith and will betray and]	hate
each other	and many false prophets	will appear and deceive
many people	because of the increase of [wickedness	
the love of most	will grow	
cold	but the one who stands firm	
to the end	will be saved	
and this gospel	of the] kingdom [will be	
preached in	the whole world as] a testimony	to
all nations	and then]	the end
will come		

Lord

Woah / the slo-mo / strobe-lit bunny / another one right behind it

I almost ran over now / stop-motion like / commotion in the dark

I'm privy to / biking again with front & back covered / white & red

flashing for all y'all / anyone in my past or my future / the beasts

& / the not yet beasting human / runners / other bikers / the flash

on & off the paused deer fam / antlers / or the Y peace sign of trees

/ nothing more the world needs than the Ridgewood Village Hall

adjacent / to the Ridgewood Library I noticed just now / all everyone

needs / is books & voices / & a quick cricket crescendo / as in film

manipulation / soundtrack of certain crises ahead / a trio of ducks

also strobe-lit waddling alongside / the bike path / let me turn off the

lights & adjust out the night world / the word night / any second

I'd pop my dark cherry wheels on / a thick femur of amputated

oak / most ferocious noise this hour remains / a garbage truck &

its jaws opening / the men & their mandibles toxic-hollering / as usual

/ even a school bus would assault my earfacing the bend / I believe

soon / that dips down under the arch of a footbridge / a brief cave

I haven't evolved enough to see inside of yet / bet / a clan of German

shepherds / bet / a booby-trap of wire one above / one below to amputate me / to decapitate me / or a nail spike rail to fuck up my

skinny tires / the flip flops now / of a girl ambling toward the coffee

shop would negate / the slow pulse / of cricket calm / this hour

of runners / deer / any shadow now could mean moose collision /

could mean the Lord / aite / I'm thinking a poem where I collide / yes

with said beast / not that we the same / stature height yea right & weight

no way / his hair / fur-style / footwear he be in his hooves / his black

platform shoes / be my image / for the Lord I've never seen / but for

Google / but for the Psalmist / in the years of captivity / Psalm eighty

verses eight through eleven / a moose / in his mouth / ripped a vine out

of Egypt / stampeding through / the camping nations / bet / drives

them settlers out / spits out / the vine onto / they campfires / Lord /

saliva-douse toward smoke & ash / settling / toward soil ready for roots

that would grow / eventually / behold / into giant Eastern red cedars.

Revelation

These humans / these eventual beasts / bet / sleeping still

in their high thread-count whites smug / in they snug soft

sheets / meanwhile / my dark bat's been up / since the sun

bled / cowered and fled from off the garden state / horizon.

I'm biking / this morning I'm thinking of the end of things

the bend at the tunneling night. They all gon flip with glee

watch / foam at the joy hole of they cake caves they white

candle teeth / lit / cheesing for they group selfie / selfie-

sticks / they gon belch with they bitch-ass bark of a beast

guffaw / they all small dog / big park-bellow snark toward

all them trees flanking the edge / of burning field / check it

yonder / them Dali-melting walls / receding borders bemoan

the sun incorrigible / rising / this hour. They is we / & we

is wild & beasting together / we varied & one / O / on that

day maybe / maybe not / you wish / ya small talking heads

for now / for he also forced everyone small & great / rich

& poor / free & [en-]slave[d] / to receive a mark on one's

right hand / or on one's forehead / so that none could buy

or sell anything unless one had the mark / which is the name of the beast / or the number of his name / [&] this calls for

wisdom [&] if anyone has insight let one calculate the number

of the beast [beasting] / for it is man's number [&] his number

is [45] / behold now / an up-turned squirrel air bicycling by

the middle yellows / writhing out his own daymare / horror.

I stall / at Hope & Ridgewood ready to loop this bike path

round these woods / the deer fam all grazing up on the path

with they no-fucks stare / no-flinches left of they dark marble

eyes / they snake-gliding / slow slithering / cross the path.

Even the Roadkill Shall Be Raised

How much raccoon doom / squirrel spaz / deer leg twitching

must we endure? I fear the ones still writhing / clawing down

the wooden Venetians for privacy / some space while dying

dignified / their rodent grills flattened on the blacktop like fresh

haemul pajun / kimchi jun / for the day of the Lord will come

like a thief in the night / the heavens will disappear with a roar /

the elements destroyed by fire / and the earth and everything

will be laid bare / the Lord is not slow in keeping his promise / as

some of you understand slowness / he is patient with you / not

wanting anyone to perish / but everyone to come to repentance

bet / even the big red-belly robins this morning / in the arboretum

weighing down limb to limb / lumbering it seems away from my

own incursion into their spaces / their there / even if I'm here

for now / never not surprised at the deer fam at the 1.2 mile marker

on the Saddle River Pathway / or / *I See You Mommy Deer with*

Your Two Daughters / not sure if there were ever a pops in the picture

but you walking off / mommy just paused / turned around / no /

body forward / turned only her head like bending an elbow / like

an eel turning to see what would thieve her tail in the cold ocean of night / O / the steam off the pond this hour like the upper room /

white tongues of flame lapping the holy morning air / high five

the low hanging leaves / watch for the roots too / the veins on them

granddaddy hands still groping towards hope / in all of us riding

in the woods before sun-up ride / with ass a little off the seat / light

on the handlebars / in the distance the wooden train clatter / horn-

warning for boats in a harbor / clear the way toward the city / whale

holler in the still dark waves of night / percussion over rails what

my finger would trace down your spine / fingernail over a comb

strumming over and over / a blue harp till you wake / love / till I

return from my morning ride singing / the last was not the scrape of

a squirrel claw / a foot kicking at the sky / was the wag of its tail

like the motion / the lightness of a wiffle ball bat from my childhood /

albino father / yo / a sighting at long last / your antlers / pincers

as wide as the width of my temples / what would pierce through me past

the beef of my useless brain / were we to collide this hour of mist

and hidden roots / the scent of threat / these taut skinny tires that would

burrow into whatever beast would cross me in the dark / any second

let me pump the brake / ease up a bit / the headwind / turn my head

a bit like an eel / a deer this hour / let me earface the future right quick.

Y'all Raking Leaves

Check these hands / these baby palms & grandma hands / arthritic-

      curve misshapen things / some older children too / tight curled

& woke into fists / here my nieces' hands & a random-ass bone /

      a bag of Cheetos / here my mother / here some hands both brown

& black from the morning dew / say / we been dying for weeks /

      for days now leafing up to this morning / y'all woke to the news

while brushing with steel fingers the wet lawn / the piles of hands

      / bones what the maple / the cherry & gingko shed / on the lawn /

the grass frizz-untangled / the shedding of skin & hair / fingernails

      down your back-scratching ooh / o yea right there / a little lower /

to the left / higher yes / right there / the rake taking the dead cells

      off your backs onto the sidewalk steel-scrape / the blacktop street

toward leaf-piles the size of parked cars / check it split pumpkins

      some flatten-smashed by tires maybe / roadkill pumpkin / earlier

this morning dear / some five of you deer / heads up gaze-frozen

      for this photo / *tchu tchu tchu* / the sucking teeth come hither sound

we make for dogs as well / *tchu tchu* / come here won't hurt you yo

      won't murder your entire fam / like we have in the past / we'll run

promise right after this pic / safely around the pond / the other

      side this arboretum / we'll see each other soon / on the news.

Knock & the Door Will Be Opened

Bouquet of letters junk

mailing a red mailbox /

house on Doremus /

the slant of lamppost

an uprooted tree / signs

of rapture or death by

the Rona / by lonely

quarantine / leaf blowers

again / their backpacks

/ their elephant trunks

heaving air-hot lies all

around / once I saw a tail

bushy-vanish into trash /

I kicked the bin to hear

the scurry I was smiling /

we've kicked a few bins

before / we men / the fog

this hour a cock crowing

its own girth / competing

the height / the visibility

of tall pines a row of cops

or firemen / the toxic fog

we've seen this before /

a squirrel in a trash bin

the hinge / the trapdoor

trapping them claws / no

moves left overnight amid

juice boxes / soda cans

& chip bags y'all nibbled at

for hours / once I heard

a scraping between ceiling

& roof / with a broom I

thrust hard & fast / knock

knocked & no one answered.

Where the Wind Sent Them Flying

After Carl Philips

Shuffle-skid down the street / scuttle-flee
                              the scene after looting for sneaks / flat screens

& other essentials / bet / yoga gear Lululemon
                              watch / slow-casual / then sprinting from them

dark helmets & visors / they sirens / yo / clear
                              the way the wind blows the brown black leaves

this hour the maple / the yellow ginkgo / others
                              inching up the street / with they children / with

they placards homemade black lives / o do they
                              do they matter now / ya plain clothes cops / ya

tone police / ya tome police / white zealots for
                              a day / put your motherfucking signs away / ya

clanging gongs in thy rooms / on thy zooms
                              yapping / decapitated things where your torsos

at / where your corsets at / one of your tribe
                              caught jacking off on a call / we read / he fled

to where the wind sent him flying / hide behind
                              a lamppost behind a tire / let it gust on through

this moment / this hate immense I thought I'd
                              have shaken off by now / by now snow season

should have been here what would keep us apart
                              for weeks / we need wider shovels / some salt

for the sidewalk / for the dead bodies what are
                              we at now / do we even care for a cure who will

be first to stab oneself / to crown oneself with
                              many crowns hark now awake our souls & sing

of all who died / of those still dying for no one.

Rorschach

See them leaving / them low gliding geese / are they back already
in January / have we been / really / for this long walking north / yo

pass me a compass / no / pass me the binocs / let me check out
them breasts / bet / as they heave on by above / that flapping

dark mass of a sky Rorschach / oval / into rectangle / trapezoidal
morph into rhombus into familiar V / some of them / check it /

as I'd never seen this before / this flap-nudge / space-checking
stay in your own lane / fool / ya too loose goose straighten up off

my line / ya flap-hazard gaggle ya drama above / then gone / & I
keep walking the trail / sudden deer skipping by / three legged

it seems / a syncopated rhythm / just a bum ankle turns out / runs
behind a red treehouse choke-holding / an oak / it's cold / I'm

thinking a warm empty diner / to sit at a two-top in some corner
by a window / order black coffee / a cheeseburger deluxe medium

rare / mozzarella melted all up on that 10 oz. tongue / thigh whatnot
flank of animal / I'll ask for ketchup & tabasco / some masked man

will point to a small bowl at my table / & there they'll be / them
ketchup packs / beside the open casket of sugar / white Dominos /

pink Sweet & Lows / them yellow Splendas stacked / them dead
bodies in freezer trucks it's that cold / in the middle of these woods

gonna kneel now in the snow / genuflect my father / myself / &
the holy geese above / dropping shit from the sky I receive as Lord /

Lord / I fear a bump on my left ball / a small cyst / says urologist
to leave it alone / deep pimple you can't pop which / after groping

for weeks / has woke-swollen into something unignorable / ignore it
you have maybe a decade left / I promise / say none of these geese.

White Noise Machine

on hurricane mode / wildfire mode / low whirlpool mode
        a pond with a little wind rippling over while underneath

a thousand tadpole / then frog-abduction tornado mode / lawn-
        chairs / lampposts ruby red slippers into sky mode / cackling

green witch mode / roofs & picket fences funneling up like
        a genie on coke mode / green garden hose in the summer

mode where we'd thumb the hole / the hiss-heaving douse
        of all our friends & if you good with all this / if you can sleep

through all this you've made it in this country / but we up
        son / something rustling in a tree by the window the wind

a branch rubbing up the side of the house / motion lights on
        & off in the yard meaning rabbit / raccoon who steps to us

at 5 AM to mob us to rob us our recycle cans / when's the blade
        coming for me / my pops shoved down hard to the ground

in his own driveway / who's spitting in my mother's eyes /
        who's gunning down my sisters this hour / white noise taking

over with their sudden fan mode / a breeze easy down a lane
        of evergreen mode / we on this trail an hour more before

sunrise / where's the bag of beef jerky / did we remember
        to bag it within a bag within another bag / to hoist it with rope

with nylon twine-high away from bears / bear vigilant mode
        deer alert mode / white noise machine / white noise /

machine white / noise machine / white noise machine I grope
        for a beanie by my pillow / pull it over my head my ears lie

face-up into snore mode sleep like I don't want to wake / white
        noise machine / white noise / machine white / noise machine.

Benediction

"Attention, taken to its highest degree,
is the same thing as prayer.
It presupposes faith and love."
                              —Simone Weil

Roach the room when the lights turn on. Remain, I mean. Do not

unsettle, scatter like cowards. Meddle
                              their minds, their meetings

and keep your shit tight, alert.
                    They'll try to heal you, to heel you,

yes, to step to you, reel
                    you in like salmon, the ones with flesh of

deeper red. Writhe not,
          ichthus. Be still   like a dying mouse on the dark

linoleum
     or a tick-riddled deer just staring, bearing your boredom.

Maverick, lone
          rabbit in the middle of a field—that woke. Like

a taxidermic fox. Like
               prayer, like absolute unmixed attention. Like

lizards on stone. Like love.

Timothy Ree is the son of Korean immigrants. He teaches literature and writing at a public high school in Brooklyn, New York. He holds a BA in English Literature from Wheaton College (IL) and an M.Div from Yale University. His poems have appeared in Tribes, Great Weather for Media, and The Cortland Review. He has received grants and fellowships from the National Endowment for the Humanities, Cave Canem, Poets House, and the Academy for Teachers. He is a recipient of the Robert Haiduke Poetry Prize from the Bread Loaf School of English.

www.ingramcontent.com/pod-product-compliance
Lightning Source LLC
Chambersburg PA
CBHW021156090426
42740CB00008B/1117